4/15

BODY
INVADERS

MATTESON PUBLIC LIBRARY

Richard Spilsbury

Enslow Publishers, Inc.
40 Industrial Road
Box 398
Berkeley Heights, NJ 07922
USA

http://www.enslow.com

This edition published by Enslow Publishers Inc.

Library of Congress Cataloging-in-Publication Data

Zoom in on body invaders / Richard Spilsbury.
     p. cm. — (Zoom in on–)
  Summary: "Get an up-close look at some of the creatures that live in and on your body"—Provided by publisher.
  ISBN 978-0-7660-4310-7
  1. Parasites—Juvenile literature. I. Title. II. Series: Spilsbury, Richard, 1963- Zoom in on–
  QR251.S73 2013
  578.6'5–dc23
                              2012045285

Future edition:
Paperback ISBN: 978-1-4644-0565-5

To Our Readers: We have done our best to make sure all Internet addresses in this book were active and appropriate when we went to press. However, the author and the publisher have no control over and assume no liability for the material available on those Internet sites or on other Web sites they may link to. Any comments or suggestions can be sent by e-mail to comments@enslow.com or to the address on the back cover.

Printed in China
122012 WKT, Shenzhen, Guangdong, China
10 9 8 7 6 5 4 3 2 1

First published in the UK in 2012 by Wayland

Wayland
338 Euston Rd
London NW1 3BH

Commissioning editor: Victoria Brooker
Project editor: Alice Harman
Designer: Paul Cherrill for Basement68
Picture research: Richard Spilsbury and Alice Harman
Proofreader and indexer: Martyn Oliver

Picture credits: 3, 7 Wikimedia/United States Department of Health and Human Services; 3 (inset), 14 (top), Shutterstock/ Cosmin Manci; 4, 16, Shutterstock/Stefan Schejok; 5, 22 (top), Dreamstime/Mirceax; 6, Science Photo Library/Jeremy Burgess; 7, Dreamstime/Kadmy; 8, Dreamstime/Ken Cole; 8 (inset), Wikimedia/United States Department of Health and Human Services; 9, Science Photo Library/David Scharf; 10 (top), Dreamstime/Miramisska; 10 (bottom), Dreamstime/Brad Calkins; 11, Science Photo Library/Steve Gschmeissner; 12, 29, Dreamstime/Andrey Armyagov; 13, Science Photo Library/ Power and Syred; 14 (bottom) Science Photo Library/Scott Camazine; 15, Science Photo Library/Eye of Science; 17 Science Photo Library/Eye of Science; 18, Science Photo Library/ Clouds Hill Imaging; 19, Corbis/ Dennis Kunkel Microscopy, Inc./Visuals Unlimited; 20, Dreamstime/Sandor Kacso; 21 (top), Science Photo Library/Manfred Kage, Peter Arnold Inc.; 21 (bottom), 28, Dreamstime/Daleen Loest; 22/23 (bottom), Shutterstock/leospek; 23 (top) Science Photo Library/Eye of Science; 24 (top), Shutterstock/D. Kucharski & K. Kucharska; 24 (bottom), Alamy/Charles O. Cecil; 25, cartercenter.org; 26 (top), Dreamstime/Msatasoy; 26 (bottom) Science Photo Library, Dr. John Brackenbury; 27, Science Photo Library/NIBSC.

CONTENTS

THE SCALE OF THINGS

We are under attack! Our bodies are ideal places for some living things to live on or in. But we cannot even see many of these invaders. Scientists need to use powerful **microscopes** to zoom in on (magnify) body invaders so they can study them.

Invisible world

It's hard to imagine how small some things really are. The smallest objects the human eye can see are about 0.2 mm long. There are 1000 **microns** to a millimeter. A human hair (with a width of about 100 microns) is huge compared to most things scientists zoom in on!

Sense of scale

A scale tells you how big something is shown, compared to its real size. This is what it means when something is said to be 25 times its actual size. You'll see scales next to many images in this book, to give you a sense of the size of objects.

This mite is
360 TIMES
its actual size

A human viewed at the same scale would be 600m (1968.5 feet) tall!

Tools of the trade

How can we zoom in on things? Light microscopes bounce light off surfaces to create images. They use **lenses** (curved pieces of glass) that bend light rays to **magnify** an image. The most powerful light microscopes can magnify things up to about 2000 times!

A light microscope.

These are salmonella bacteria (colored pink), seen under a microscope.

Scanning electron microscopes (SEMs)

These microscopes use electrons instead of light. Electrons are tiny parts inside **atoms**. SEMs bounce electrons off surfaces to create images. Electron microscopes can magnify things by almost a million times!

Fearsome fact

Animals that live on others to get food and shelter without giving anything in return are called **parasites**.

7

BED BUGS GET BITING

No one is safe! It doesn't matter if you're in a five-star hotel or a dirty room with clothes and crumbs on the floor. Bed bugs can be found anywhere that people are sleeping.

Bedtime attack

Bed bugs are tiny, flat **insects**. They come out at night to suck on a sleeping person's blood. Then they scurry back to hide in places like bed frames, carpets, or cracks in the floor or walls.

Bed bugs grow to 4–5 mm long, but they're rarely seen as they hide in the daytime.

Fearsome fact

Bed bugs are hard to get rid of because they can live for up to a year without feeding!

New York nightmare

In 2010, bed bugs invaded the city of New York, NY. The bed bugs were everywhere—in hotels, homes, schools, movie theaters, stores and offices. Newspapers called it a "Blood Bug Invasion"!

8

Don't let the bed bugs bite!

A bed bug cannot fly. It senses a person's body heat and climbs up to feed. Then it sticks its sharp **proboscis** into their skin and injects **saliva** (spit) into the wound. This liquid contains an **anaesthetic** so the victim doesn't feel the bite. It also stops the blood clotting so the bug can keep on feeding for up to ten minutes. As the little monster fills with blood, it changes color from brown to red!

Bed bug bites don't hurt, but they leave red blotches that itch for days!

proboscis

This bed bug is
110
TIMES
its actual size

KNOW YOUR FOE
Check cracks and crevices, and your bed and mattress. Look for bed bugs, blood spots or dark feces spots on sheets, walls and carpets. If you see signs like these, call in the exterminator!

9

LICE ON THE LOOSE

Warning! It will be hard to read about this beast without scratching your head! Head lice are tiny, wingless insects that live on human hair. They feed on blood several times a day.

Itchy invaders

Itching is often the first sign of head lice. These creepy crawlers only suck tiny amounts of blood but they also inject some of their saliva, which is what makes people itch. Lice are hard to spot because, although they cannot hop or fly, they crawl quickly. Head lice need human blood to survive. Once removed from a head, they starve in one or two days.

Adult lice are 1–3 mm long – that's about the size of a sesame seed!

KNOW YOUR FOE

Head lice love all hair —long, short, dirty or clean! They crawl from person to person when heads touch. To get rid of head lice, use a special lotion and comb you can buy at a pharmacy.

Look out for lice

Close-up, the first thing you notice about a head louse is its huge claws! These help it cling onto human hair and crawl about to feed and to lay eggs. Female head lice lay eggs, or nits, that are smaller than a pinhead. They glue the eggs to the base of a hair. The temperature here is just right for keeping eggs warm until they hatch. The eggs hatch after seven to ten days. After another ten days, these young lice become adults and they start laying eggs too!

Head lice have a large, hook-like claw on each of their six legs.

This head louse is **80 TIMES** its actual size

Fearsome fact

Head lice live for about 30 days on a head if left untreated.

Eyelash Bugs

Not all body invaders are bad news. Some can be helpful, like follicle mites. **Follicles** are tiny holes in your skin from which hairs grow. Follicle mites living in these holes help keep the follicles clean!

Living in your lashes

Follicle mites usually live on the face, and often in the roots of eyelashes! The mites stay head-down in a follicle, feeding on dead skin **cells** and on an oily substance called sebum. This oil is released by glands near the follicle to moisturize and protect skin and hair.

Follicle mites are so tiny that people never even know they are there!

Fearsome fact

Children have very few follicle mites. You tend to get more as you get older—so almost all older adults have them!

Good news!

You'll be pleased to know that the mite's **digestive system** is so efficient that it doesn't make any waste. So mites in eyelashes never produce mite droppings!

Follicle-fitting features

Eyelash mites look a bit like insects, but they have four pairs of legs instead of three. Their long, thin body helps them to fit inside narrow hair follicles. Their legs are all up at the head end. Up to 25 mites can fit in one follicle! When it gets too crowded, a mite uses its legs to drag the rest of its body to a new follicle. Follicle mites feed using their tiny claws and needle-like **mouthparts**.

Follicle mites have scales all over their body, to help anchor them in the hair follicles!

KNOW YOUR FOE

Follicle mites can be passed from person to person on towels and other fabrics, so one way to avoid mites is to avoid sharing these things.

This follicle mite is **1860 TIMES** its actual size

Hop Aboard the Flea Express

A few centuries ago, almost everyone was covered in little red itchy bumps from human flea bites. Today the human flea mostly lives on pigs and some other animals, but it still likes the taste of human blood when it can get it!

A flea's long and springy back legs help it leap aboard its victims!

Filling up fleas

Human fleas have a small head and a large abdomen, or stomach. This gets bigger to hold more blood when the flea feeds! This flea is a nuisance because the saliva in its bite makes people itch, and it can also pass on diseases from other animals.

Champion jumper

A human flea can leap 30 cm (12 in)—that's 200 times its own height! If you could do that, you could jump over the Eiffel Tower in Paris, France!

Fearsome fact

A flea has backward-pointing hairs all over its body, which help it to cling to a victim's skin.

Flea bites are itchy, but it's important not to scratch them as they can get infected.

14

Human fleas like this are found all over the world!

eye

This human flea is **430 TIMES** its actual size

palp

mouthparts

Fearsome flea!

When you zoom in on a flea's head, it looks pretty fearsome! The flea's pointed head and flat body help it to move quickly through human body hair. Its eyes are quite large so it can see at day and night. It has sticking-out parts called palps around its mouth, which are used for feeling and tasting. They test whether something they touch is food or not. Between the palps, you can see the mouthparts that pierce human skin and greedily suck blood.

TICKS LATCH ON

When you take a pleasant walk in a forest, field, or park you might come home with an unwanted guest. That small black spot on your ankle may be a blood-sucking tick!

Ticked off?

Ticks live in grass, bushes and fallen leaves. They wait for a person or animal to pass by, then they stretch out their front legs and use tiny hooks on the legs to latch on to a foot or ankle. They bite into the skin and start to feed. If undisturbed, they will feed for around five to seven days before letting go and dropping off!

When ticks feed they increase in weight by up to 200 times. That's when people can see them!

Tick terrors

Tick saliva contains bacteria that can spread diseases, such as Lyme disease. Lyme disease is nasty and causes **fever**, and muscle and joint pain, so anyone who feels unwell after being bitten by a tick should see a doctor.

Fearsome fact

To avoid tick attacks, wear shoes rather than sandals and tuck long pants into socks.

Ticks look fierce close up, but their bites don't hurt.

chelicerae

palps for tasting

hypostome

This tick is
225 TIMES
its actual size

Tick attack!

Face to face with a tick you can see how its attack is so effective! The chelicerae mouthparts at the center of its face are like sharp scissors. The tick uses these to cut a hole in the skin. Then it plunges its long hypostome into the skin. This part has backward-pointing spikes that anchor the animal in the skin and make it hard to get out. Once this tube is firmly anchored in place, the tick also uses it to suck up blood.

KNOW YOUR FOE

You've got to remove a tick in one piece, so it doesn't release more saliva or its stomach contents into your bite wound! With pointed tweezers, grasp the tick as close to the skin as possible without squeezing its body, then pull it out slowly without twisting.

17

GUT-SQUATTING WORMS

Without knowing it, people in some parts of the world carry around tapeworms deep inside their bodies. These long, flat worms are parasites that live in human intestines.

A worm's life

Tapeworms absorb nutrients from the soup of digesting food that constantly washes over them in the intestines. People may know they have tapeworms because they are losing weight—that's because the worms are taking the nutrients from their food!

Tapeworms' bodies are like thin, tapering ribbons of tagliatelle divided into segments. Segments at the end of their body contain eggs. These segments break off and are released in feces (poo) to spread the eggs.

segments

end

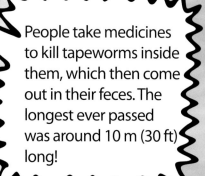

People take medicines to kill tapeworms inside them, which then come out in their feces. The longest ever passed was around 10 m (30 ft) long!

KNOW YOUR FOE

People may get a tapeworm by accidentally eating its eggs. These can get onto fingers and under fingernails from soil, clothing or on animal's fur. Wash your hands before eating!

hook

sucker

Holding on

Tapeworms need to stay put in the intestine so they can feed. They do this by pushing their head into the intestine wall. Suckers and sharp hooks coming out of the head help them to hold on, and escape being washed out by the digesting food.

This tapeworm is **40 TIMES** its actual size

Fearsome fact

There are around 6000 species of tapeworm. More than 50 different types of tapeworm live in humans!

TOOTH ATTACK

We have swarms of bacteria all over our bodies, inside and out. They get inside us on food we eat, air we breathe in, or through cuts in skin. Many of these microscopic living things, or **microorganisms**, are very useful, but some make us sick or cause us harm.

Bacteria feast

Your mouth makes a great place for bacteria to grow. They collect in the dips and cracks in the surface of teeth. These bacteria make plaque, the sticky yellow substance that forms a layer over teeth.

When bacteria digest the bits of food in our mouth they also make acids. The combination of sticky plaque and acid is what causes tooth decay.

Open wide! Have bacteria covered your teeth in plaque?

Fearsome fact

There are around 1 billion bacteria on every tooth!

KNOW YOUR FOE

Streptococcus mutans is hard to get rid of. Your best bet is to reduce the amount of sugary food you eat and clean your teeth well twice a day to remove the bits of food from which it gets sugar. Without sugar, bacteria can't make so much plaque or acid.

These bacteria are **23,000 TIMES** their actual size

Sinister *streptococcus*

Streptococcus mutans is the main culprit for tooth decay. Once inside your mouth, these beastly bacteria stick to teeth and feed on the bits of food wedged between them. When these bacteria digest sucrose sugar in food, they create plaque. When they digest other sugars, like fructose in fruit and lactose in cheese, they produce acid.

Acids in plaque break down a tooth's enamel surface and make holes like this.

MOSQUITO HIJACKERS

Some tiny parasites invade human bodies by hitching a lift from other creatures. Mosquitoes in some parts of the world, including most African countries, pass on tiny malaria parasites when they bite people.

Only female mosquitoes are bloodthirsty. Males have short mouths that can't pierce skin.

Takeaway delivery

A female mosquito needs to eat blood to make her eggs grow. She flies around to find a victim, and then plunges her long mouthparts into skin to drink her fill. But while her mouth is busy, parasites in her gut swim out and into the victim's blood.

In the Amazon Rainforest, people sleep under nets so mosquitoes can't feast on them in the night.

Fearsome fact

It is difficult to hide from a mosquito. It can smell breath or sweat from up to 36 m (100 ft) away.

KNOW YOUR FOE

People reduce their chances of catching malaria by keeping mosquitoes at bay. They sleep under mosquito nets, wear long sleeves, and protect their skin with chemicals called insect repellents.

Inside job

Once inside the body, the parasites move into red blood cells where they feed, breed and grow in numbers. This makes blood cells swell until they burst and release more parasites into the blood.

Bursting cells cause fevers and sweating that can be severe enough to kill people, especially weaker young and old people.

Malaria parasites (yellow) attacking red blood cells. When their red blood cells are damaged by malaria, people can become dangerously ill or even die.

These parasites are **8600 TIMES** their actual size

Staying safe

People should take anti-malarial drugs when visiting places where mosquitoes spread malaria. These kill some of the parasites if they do get bitten.

23

WORMS UNDER THE SKIN

Drinking water in some parts of Africa has a major health warning— it might contain tiny guinea worms. Once these parasites get inside your body, they grow bigger and bigger, and eventually get out by burrowing through your skin!

Getting inside

Young guinea worm larvae usually live inside small water fleas found in lakes and rivers. When people drink the water, the fleas get into their digestive system. Strong chemicals in the intestine kill the flea, but the worms emerge safe and sound. They burrow into spaces in flesh around the intestine, where they feed and grow into adults. Males are much smaller than females, and die after mating.

A water flea is almost transparent, so with a microscope you can see its insides!

Taking water samples from lakes and rivers allows people to study guinea worms.

KNOW YOUR FOE

People avoid catching guinea worm by drinking water through straws that filter out the fleas!

24

Painful journey

Female guinea worms travel through their victim's flesh in order to have their young. They chomp and wriggle toward the skin on the belly or legs, causing great pain to their host. A blister forms on the skin where the worm has reached the surface.

People often go into water to soothe the burning pain of guinea worm blisters. This is what the female wants. The blister pops, she pokes her head out, and releases hundreds of **larvae** that swim away.

A doctor can help to safely get a guinea worm out of a person's body.

Gently does it

Victims of guinea worms don't dare to pull at the emerging parasite because it could break, die and rot inside their flesh. They gently wind worms around sticks to get them out faster, but it may still take weeks!

Fearsome fact

Guinea worms are the thickness of paper clip wire and females can reach over 1 m (3 ft) in length.

VIRUSES HITCH A RIDE

Viruses are even smaller than bacteria. In fact, they are the smallest microorganisms that can invade a body. Viruses give people diseases like colds, flu and measles.

Viruses on the move

Viruses can move quickly from person to person. People breathe them in from the air, for example after someone who has the flu sneezes. People accidentally pick up virus particles on their fingers when they touch a surface, such as a door knob, that has been contaminated by someone who has the flu. The virus gets inside the body when the person touches their nose, eyes or mouth.

Catch it—throw it out—kill it!

Reduce the spread of cold, flu and other viruses. Catch your sneezes in a tissue, and throw out the tissue right away. Then wash your hands to kill any virus particles left on your fingers.

Fearsome fact

A sneeze can carry around 200 million viruses!

A single sneeze can fill the air in a room with cold or flu viruses.

This virus is attacking red blood cells.

red blood cell

virus

Virus villains

When viruses get inside a body, they start to attack healthy cells. Flu virus cells have a covering of minuscule spikes that help them cling to individual cells. Viruses cannot reproduce by themselves like bacteria.

They have to move inside the cell, and use the cell to make more viruses. The viruses eventually kill the cell they have been using. The new viruses leave and attach to other, healthy cells, and infect them too.

KNOW YOUR FOE

Many bacterial infections can be treated with **antibiotics**, but these are useless against viruses. You can be vaccinated against some disease-causing viruses, like the flu. You just have to wait to recover from others, such as the cold virus.

Glossary

anaesthetic–chemical that stops someone from feeling pain, for example when an insect bites or when having an operation

bacteria–simple and tiny living things that live in air, water, soil and other living things

cell–the smallest, most basic unit from which all living things are made

digestive system–set of organs, including mouth and stomach, that help animals process and get nutrients from food

fever–when someone has higher than normal body temperature, which can be dangerous if not reduced

follicle–tiny hole in skin through which hairs grow

insect–type of small animal usually with three body sections and six legs, and often with wings

intestine–long tube connecting the stomach and bottom in the digestive system

larvae–young hatched from eggs of certain types of animals including insects, fish, and frogs

lens–curved piece of glass that bends light rays; used in microscopes and magnifying glasses

magnify–make bigger; enlarge

malaria–dangerous and often deadly disease of tropical countries caused by a parasite and spread by mosquitoes

micron–unit of measurement equal to one-millionth of a meter; 12 microns is about half the width of a human hair

microorganism–tiny living thing such as a bacterium and virus so small it can only be seen through a microscope

microscope–device that produces enlarged images of objects that are normally too small to be seen

mouthparts–parts of the mouth in different animals, ranging from lips and mandibles to pincers and jaws

parasite–living thing that lives on or in another to feed or benefit in other ways, usually harming the host (the living thing it uses) in the process

proboscis–long narrow mouth, often shaped like a tube or needle to suck blood or other fluids

saliva–fluid produced in the mouth to help swallow food; also called spit

virus–simple microorganism that invades other organisms and lives on or in their cells, where it can increase in number

Books

From Armpits to Zits: The Book of Yucky Body Bits by Paul Mason (Wayland, 2011)

Insect Investigators: Entomologists (Scientists at work) by Richard and Louise Spilsbury (Heinemann, 2008)

Malaria: Super Killer! (Nightmare Plagues) by Stephen Person (Bearport, 2010)

Microscopic Life by Richard Walker (Kingfisher, 2004)

Tapeworms, Foot Fungus, Lice, and More: The Yucky Disease Book (Yucky Science) by Alvin Silverstein, Virginia Silverstein and Lara Silverstein Nunn (Enslow, 2010)

The World of the Microscope (Usborne Science and Experiments) by Chris Oxlade and Corinne Stockley (Usborne, 2008)

Websites

Could you become a disease detective using microscopes and other technology to zap the microorganisms that cause them? Visit <www.diseasedetectives.org> to learn more, including interviews with real-life scientists.

Explore the remarkable world of viruses through images, radio clips, apps, and comics at <www.worldofviruses.unl.edu /index> Check out the Frozen Horror comic about the flu virus!

Malaria is a devastating disease in many countries. Discover facts and figures about this disease, and how people are preventing its spread. Go to <www.cdc.gov/malaria/references_resources/kid_stuff.html>

Visit <http://kidshealth.org/Search01.jsp> to discover more about parasites and where they live.

INDEX

Zoom In On...

Contents of titles in the series

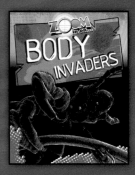

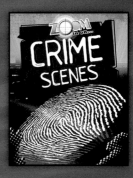

E